I AM AMAZING

workbook

FOR TEENS

By Blythe Metz–Mändmets, PhD

BLYTHE
Natural Living

BlytheNaturalLiving.com

Published by BNL Press

Los Angeles, Ca 90036

Library of Congress Cataloging-in-Publication Data

979-8-89217-242-4

Printed in USA

For information regarding bulk purchases, please visit
www.BlytheNaturalLiving.com/Store

Cover Design by Christine Leakey, www.christineleakey.com

Interior Design by Christine Leakey, www.christineleakey.com

First Edition: December 2023

Visit our website at www.BlytheNaturalLiving.com

Acknowledgments

I am first and foremost grateful to you, the reader, for taking this journey to discover your greatest talents, joys, and innate genius. I extend my deepest gratitude for allowing me to be a part of your quest to uncover the profound ways in which you will contribute your innate genius to the world. Your commitment to this transformative exploration fills me with joy and purpose. I am incredibly fortunate to have worked alongside the immensely talented Christine Leakey, whose beautiful illustrations breathe life into the pages of this workbook, making the journey within it visually inspiring. Special thanks to Sara Sardar from CM Graphics Hub for her invaluable contribution in formatting this paperback and ebook version. Their collaborative efforts have enriched this project beyond measure, and I am truly grateful for the artistry and expertise they have brought to this endeavor.

With heartfelt thanks,

Dr. Blythe

CONTENTS

Dear Teenager,
YOU ARE AMAZING.

This workbook is about helping you see your natural talents, abilities, and preferences while giving you powerful tools to create whatever you want in life. It gives you a framework to envision your greatest life expressions. It will give you your Ideal Self Blueprint.

You can have, do, and be anything if you are willing to believe in yourself and persevere when things are challenging. Know this, things will get challenging on the road to creating an amazing life. You will stumble, and there will be "failures," which aren't actually failures, as much as they are teachers that lift you higher. We learn so much from making mistakes. I wish someone would have told me to have fun failing, to learn from it, and to allow it to serve me. I let failures waste my time and energy because I didn't have anyone coaching me that I should expect to fail, and that failure is valuable feedback. So, I'm here to coach you. Failure is part of great success. Everyone who has ever created anything amazing has failed many times on the way to success. Edison failed to create a lightbulb one thousand times before he figured it out. Failure is our teacher.

In my teens, no one told me that my thoughts, energy, feelings and focus create my reality. Where would I be now if I knew that in my teens and twenties? I was in my forties before I understood the difference between being in a creative-structure in consciousness and being in a problem-solving structure (most adults never learn this so I'm grateful to have this understanding). I discuss what that means in detail in Chapter 2 of *Dear Teenager, You Are Amazing, 5 Keys to Creating a Life You Love.* You want to always be in a creative-structure, creating what you want. Not in a problem-solving structure, because inherent in a problem-solving structure is 'the problem.' We are always creating what we are conscious of being. Keeping our consciousness on the end results we want instead of on the problems we want to fix, is a massive key to creating flow in your life.

 It's quite amazing how learning a few pieces of wisdom in your teenage years can and will catapult you forward in life. I spent the last 20 years learning what I'm made of. I hope to save you lots of time so you can start creating your life in your authentically beautiful way now. You have something amazing to offer. You have everything you need to live your greatest life and accomplish your dreams. The information and inspiration you have available to you is truly remarkable. Technology has given you access to any information you desire, and that's powerful. I've heard it said that we all have access to more information in our pockets than the president of the United States did in the 1990s (Bill Clinton).

With this technology also comes exposure to things that young minds and hearts may be traumatized by, as well as additional social pressure. We are seeing more depression, anxiety, and suicide in teenagers than ever before. Learning unconditional self-love and unconditional forgiveness is the medicine and the power. These are tools to self-actualize into the amazing person that you already are, regardless of your current environment.

If you haven't already, please read the accompanying book, *Dear Teenager, You Are Amazing, 5 Keys to Creating a Life You Love*. There you will learn more about Unconditional Self-Love, The Art of Conscious Creation, Unconditional Forgiveness and so much more.

Get your favorite pen and enjoy the queries. Allow yourself to stream-of-thought write, don't censor yourself in any way. Don't worry about proper grammar. There are no wrong answers. These questions are designed to open your mind and heart. You will see maps and structures that will guide you in creating a brilliant life. Ask yourself the following questions and let the answers flow. Enjoy the process.

What are 5 things I enjoy doing?

1

2

3

4

5

What are 5 things I am naturally good at?
(may be some of the same things as question #1)

1

2

3

4

5

I have $30 million in the bank, how do I spend my days? Who do I want to spend my days with? Where do I want to contribute my time, talents and money to better other people's lives?

How much money would I like to make annually in my 20s? In my 30s? 40s? 50s? 60s? 70s and beyond?

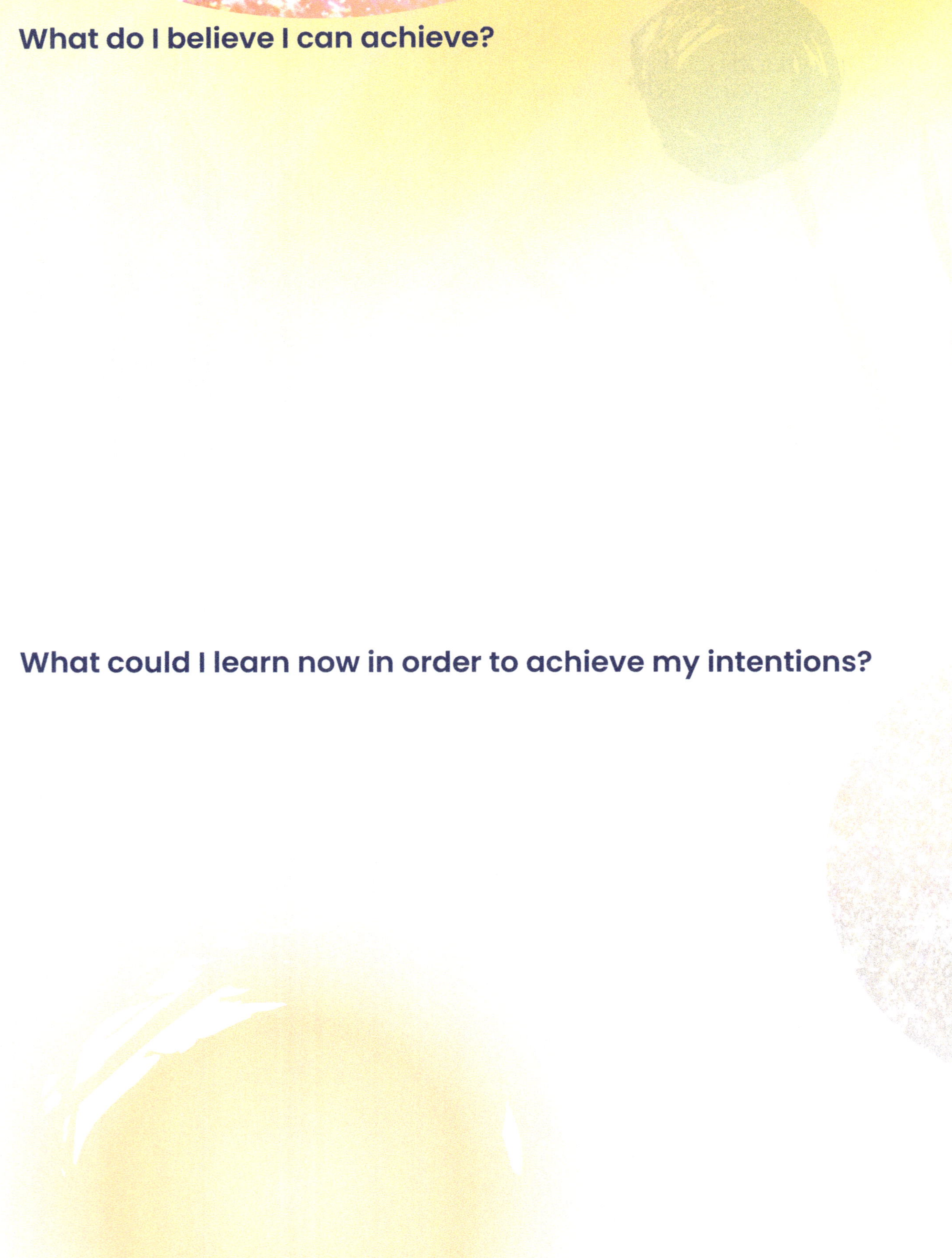

What do I believe I can achieve?

What could I learn now in order to achieve my intentions?

What do I believe I can achieve?

Where might I learn this information?

Who do I allow to influence me now? What podcasts do I listen to? What videos do I watch? Who do I spend my time listening to, observing and why?

Who do I want to influence me? Who would inspire me and pump me up if I allowed myself the time to watch a video or listen to a podcast by this person? List as many people or brands that come to mind.

What personal habits do I have that I am proud of?

If I had to describe myself in one word, what would that word be? And why?

UNCONDITIONAL FORGIVENESS

Forgiveness can feel uncertain or even wrong sometimes when the act or behavior is "unforgivable". Forgiveness is not about condoning the behavior of others. Instead forgiveness is about setting yourself free. You can set yourself free by understanding that whomever harmed you, did so from a very broken place.

Forgiveness is a power position. You have all the cards. You forgave. Truly forgave. There is an old adage that states "you can forgive but you don't have to forget." That's wrong. True forgiveness is actually forgetting. To discern however, forgetting doesn't mean you allow someone who has harmed you to do it again because you have forgotten. To forgive, we must forget because holding on to any thought of something that needs to be forgiven means it's not actually forgiven. It's got a hold of you somewhere, it's plugged into you somewhere. So you forgive and forget, while taking a very strong stance of unconditional self love.

"What do I need to forgive?

Who do I need to forgive?

What do I need to forgive myself for?

For everything you wrote down when answering the above three questions, use the following statements to clear the energy and allow forgiveness.

"I release you, this is forgiven"

Or

"I release you, you are forgiven"

Or

"I release this, this is forgiven"

Do these statements as many times as it takes to feel you have released anger, resentment or sadness.

When things come up in the future, do this work to release the trigger.
This tool will literally keep you healthy and sexy your entire very long life,
because holding onto unforgiveness weakens the immune response, therefore weakening the body.
Also holding on to "stuff' keeps you plugged into the past, instead of your brilliant NOW moment and blossoming future.

What does unconditional self love look like for me? How do I show myself love, acceptance, compassion and forgiveness now?

***The more you can show yourself love, acceptance, compassion and forgiveness, the more you will be able to show up for others in this way. This is what creates amazing relationships that enrich your life.**

CREATING YOUR IDEAL SELF BLUEPRINT

This exercise is explained in much greater detail in the accompanying book, *Dear Teenger, You Are Amazing, 5 Keys to Creating a Life You Love.* However I wanted to include this profound exercise in the workbook as well, because this is such a beautiful space to write out your Ideals in each area of your life.

The idea here is to write down what you really want in the 6 areas of life listed on the next 6 pages. Write out everything you'd like to experience and create in all these main areas of life. This gives you your Ideal Self Blueprint, which will become your life with conscious cultivation. You can't create what you want if you don't clearly identify what you want. This exercise helps you do that, AND, if you practice it the way it's laid out for you here, it will build the neural networks in your brain to match your Ideals.

A very important key to making this exercise effective, is FEELing the Ideals as you write them down. When you are writing down what you want to create in each area of life, see if you can feel what it feels like to have already created that. For instance, in the Finances section, say you write down, 'Always have more money than I need to do everything I want." Take a few minutes to feel what it feels like to always have more money than you need to do absolutely everything you need and desire to do. That will feel pretty terrific, make sure to get yourself feeling terrific.

Another example, in the Relationships section, say you write down, 'Have a great group of friends that all bring each other up,' take a few minutes to feel what that feels like to be surrounded by supportive, kind, amazing friends. I have given you a full page for each section, so write everything and anything your heart desires. Let your stream of thought flow. There is nothing too big. If you want to be a millionaire or billionaire, write it down. If you want to live somewhere obscure, write it down. If you want to be a rockstar, moviestar, or athlete, write it down. If you want to be the best parent to a house full of kiddoes, write it down. If you want to invent something that solves a problem, write it down. If you want to travel the world taking photographs, write it down. This is all about YOU, so don't be shy here. Let it really rip with your heart's desires. Go Big!

The truth is, if it's in your heart, it's meant for you. If something is in your heart to create or contribute or explore or invent, that's your higher self communicating with you what your purpose is. It's guidance. Guiding you to your promised land, AKA, a happy fulfilled life.

After completing the 6 categories, read over everything you have written and take time to FEEL all of it.

You will notice that at the bottom of each of the 6 segment pages there is a section for you to write the thoughts and feelings that you DON'T want to think and feel. These thoughts and feelings are also very important to identify because when you become familiar with how you don't want to feel and think, those thoughts and feelings will not go by you unnoticed. You will notice them. When you notice you are feeling or thinking something that you don't want to be feeling and thinking, you can at that very moment choose the Ideal thoughts and feelings from the top of the page to cultivate. This prunes the neural networks in your brain that have habituated the disempowering thoughts and feelings and by choosing to purposely FEEL your Ideals in that area of life, you will be literally rewiring your brain, creating a new mind. This is called neural plasticity and it's another one of your superpowers. Be sure to read the accompanying book *Dear Teenager, You Are Amazing, 5 Keys to Creating a Life You Love* to learn about all of your innate superpowers.

BODY

Body ~ Write all of your ideals in your physical health. Example: Run a marathon, do a backflip, heal from a diagnosis, heal my allergies, love my body, love my hair, have healthy skin, feel strong, etc.

How do I not want to feel in reference to my body?

What do I not want to think?

MIND

Mind ~ Write how you want to feel emotionally every day. What thoughts do you want to think every day?

How do I not want to feel emotionally?

What do I not want to think?

RELATIONSHIPS

Relationships ~ Write how you want to feel in your relationships. How do you want to feel in your relationship with your parents, siblings, significant other, teachers, friends, peers, etc. Write down what's important to you in friendships and how you want to show up for others. Write down what's important to you in a romantic relationship.

How do I not want to feel in my relationships?

What do I not want to think about my relationships?

FINANCES

Finances ~ What would you like your relationship with money to feel like? What do you want to do that costs money? Write down all of your ideals when it comes to money. Write down vacations you want to take, movies you want to make, whatever you want that costs money. Here is a wonderful opportunity to get it all down on paper and have a look at your Ideals with money. There is nothing too big. If it's in your heart, write it down. Remember to FEEL these things as you're writing them down. FEEL them as if you already have all the means to do them.

How do I not want to feel with my finances?

What do I not want to think about money?

CREATIVE EXPRESSION

Creative Expression ~ Write down what you want to create. This can be artistic expression or it can be simply what you want to create, like a vacation or new kicks, or a new best friend. It's okay to have repetition here from other categories, as everything you are writing down in this exercise is considered something you are creating. Have fun with this. Don't censor yourself. Go!

How do I not want to feel in reference to my creative expression?

What do I not want to think about my creative expressions?

MOVEMENT

Movement ~ This may have some repetition from the Body section, but I like to put movement separately because it's a huge aspect to a healthy happy life. Here you will write how you want to move your physical body. For example, On my Movement page, I have written 'Dancing, Boxing, Swimming, Pilates, Soccer, Hiking, Walking, Yoga, Breathwork, Thi Chi, Martial Arts, Gymnastics". Close your eyes and FEEL your body moving in the ways you write down. Studies show that muscles fire in the brain the exact same way they would if they were actually moving. Mental rehearsal is a very powerful way to become a champion athlete, all the champion athletes know this and use mental rehearsal daily. It's also a powerful way to heal the body from injury. Use this amazing superpower to strengthen your mind-body connection. Have fun with this movement section. Go!

How do I not want to feel in reference to my physical movement?

What do I not want to think about my physical movement?

YOUR MORNING ROUTINE

Use this Ideal Self Blueprint every morning when you wake up to get you connected to your vision for yourself. Feel what you have written every single day. Before long, you will see what you have written on these pages come into your life experience. It's not magic, it's the design of life...which actually is pretty magical.

You are always creating what you are conscious of being. When you do this exercise, you become conscious of being your ideals. You consciously cultivate your ideals, with repetition and deep emotion, your subconscious starts to believe these ideals are you, and your reticular activating system in your brain makes you aware of opportunities that match that ideal. Read my book, *Dear Teenager, You Are Amazing, 5 Keys to Creating a Life You Love* for a more detailed explanation of how this exercise powerfully creates your life. An entire chapter is dedicated to Imagineering-The Art of Conscious Creation.

*Write down the ways you will own yourself that make you feel empowered. Feel yourself embodying this for at least five minutes, then write down any insights that came to you. For instance, choose to own that you already possess the power within you to create whatever you want in life and that the seeds of greatness are indeed within you. Then, close your eyes, take a deep breath, and FEEL what that feels like. Embody that truth. How does it feel? Write it down.

After reading the chapter of Unconditional Self Love in *Dear Teenager, You Are Amazing, 5 Keys to Creating a Life You Love*, answer the following questions.

Am I willing to cultivate a greater unconditional self-love?

What does unconditional self-love mean to me?

What can my unconditional self-love create in my life?

How might practicing unconditional self-love improve my immediate environment?

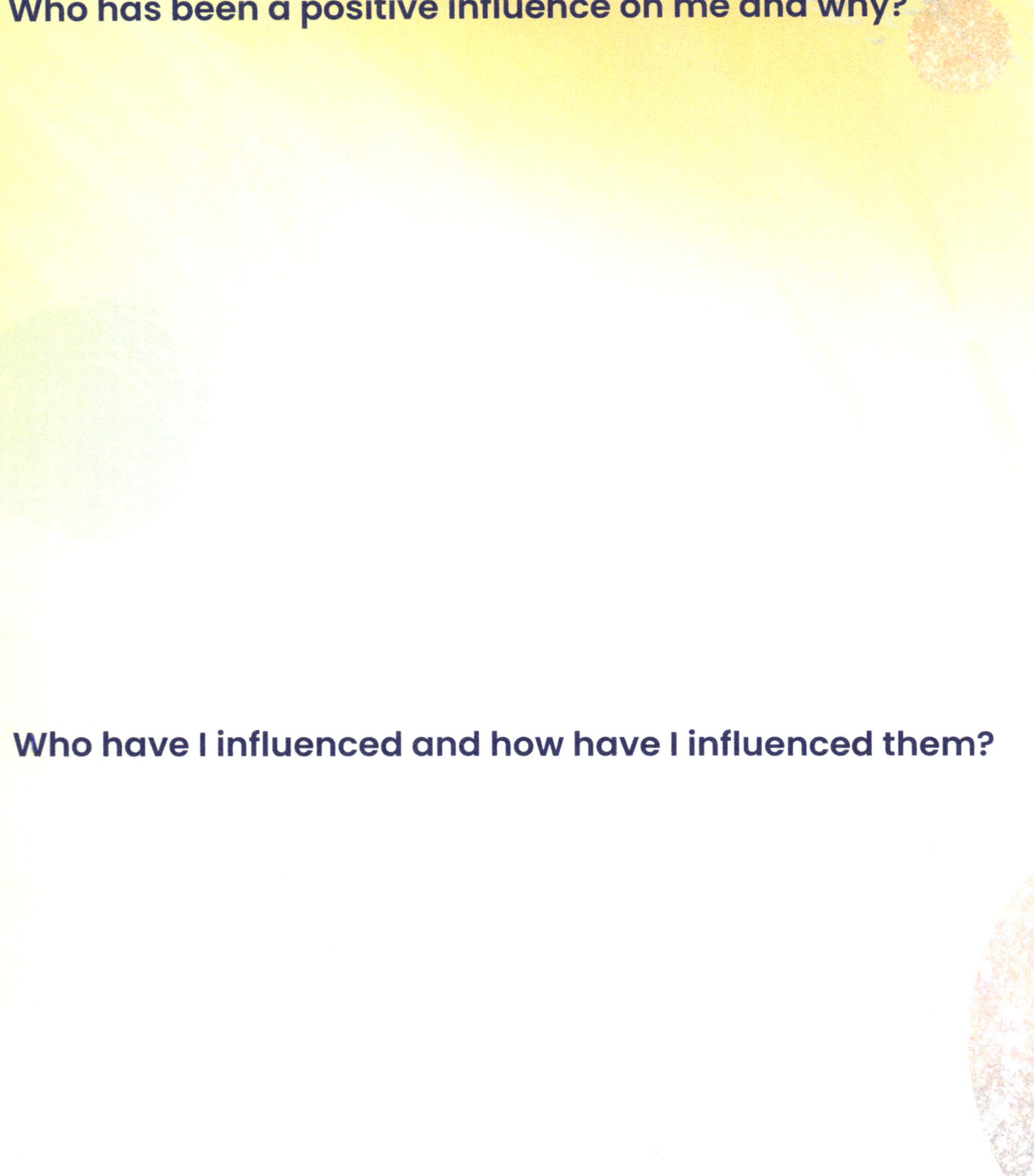

Who has been a positive influence on me and why?

Who have I influenced and how have I influenced them?

How could I be a more positive influence in the lives of those around me?

What is the greatest expression of myself that I can live today?

How can I be even more aligned with my Ideal Self?

How can I express God (ultimate love and creatorship) today?

CELEBRATE!

YOU JUST CREATED YOUR LIFE BLUEPRINT.

This is a tool to show you, yourself. This blueprint can change as often as you want to change or upgrade something. Refer to this blueprint daily, to instill the attitudes, disciplines, and energy you want as your primary experience. You really can create it the way you want it, however your sustained vibrational match to what you want must be achieved, and that's a skill. It's the skill of looking beyond present circumstances or environment and holding steadfast to your vision in present time. This workbook helps you do that. You have a HUGE advantage over most generations past, in that you have all information, (basically), available to you. AND you can choose to be influenced by amazing people in action oriented ways. It's a great time to be young! You are positioned for true greatness.

Sending you much love

Dr. Blythe

Date __/__/__

Take a deep breath, connect with Source and ask:

How do I need to BE to show up as my Ideal Self today?

What do I need to do to show up as my Ideal Self today?

Take a deep breath, connect with Source and ask:

How do I need to BE to show up as my Ideal Self today?

What do I need to do to show up as my Ideal Self today?

Date __/__/__

Take a deep breath, connect with Source and ask:

How do I need to BE to show up as my Ideal Self today?

What do I need to do to show up as my Ideal Self today?

Take a deep breath, connect with Source and ask:

How do I need to BE to show up as my Ideal Self today?

What do I need to do to show up as my Ideal Self today?

Date __/__/__

Take a deep breath, connect with Source and ask:

How do I need to BE to show up as my Ideal Self today?

What do I need to do to show up as my Ideal Self today?

Take a deep breath, connect with Source and ask:

How do I need to BE to show up as my Ideal Self today?

What do I need to do to show up as my Ideal Self today?

Date __/__/__

Take a deep breath, connect with Source and ask:

How do I need to BE to show up as my Ideal Self today?

What do I need to do to show up as my Ideal Self today?

Take a deep breath, connect with Source and ask:

How do I need to BE to show up as my Ideal Self today?

What do I need to do to show up as my Ideal Self today?

Date __/__/__

Take a deep breath, connect with Source and ask:

How do I need to BE to show up as my Ideal Self today?

What do I need to do to show up as my Ideal Self today?

Take a deep breath, connect with Source and ask:

How do I need to BE to show up as my Ideal Self today?

What do I need to do to show up as my Ideal Self today?

Date __/__/__

Take a deep breath, connect with Source and ask:

How do I need to BE to show up as my Ideal Self today?

What do I need to do to show up as my Ideal Self today?

Take a deep breath, connect with Source and ask:

How do I need to BE to show up as my Ideal Self today?

What do I need to do to show up as my Ideal Self today?

Date __/__/__

Take a deep breath, connect with Source and ask:

How do I need to BE to show up as my Ideal Self today?

What do I need to do to show up as my Ideal Self today?

Take a deep breath, connect with Source and ask:

How do I need to BE to show up as my Ideal Self today?

What do I need to do to show up as my Ideal Self today?

Date __/__/__

Take a deep breath, connect with Source and ask:

How do I need to BE to show up as my Ideal Self today?

What do I need to do to show up as my Ideal Self today?

Take a deep breath, connect with Source and ask:

How do I need to BE to show up as my Ideal Self today?

What do I need to do to show up as my Ideal Self today?

Date __/__/__

Take a deep breath, connect with Source and ask:

How do I need to BE to show up as my Ideal Self today?

What do I need to do to show up as my Ideal Self today?

Take a deep breath, connect with Source and ask:

How do I need to BE to show up as my Ideal Self today?

What do I need to do to show up as my Ideal Self today?

Date __/__/__

Take a deep breath, connect with Source and ask:

How do I need to BE to show up as my Ideal Self today?

What do I need to do to show up as my Ideal Self today?

Take a deep breath, connect with Source and ask:

How do I need to BE to show up as my Ideal Self today?

What do I need to do to show up as my Ideal Self today?

Date __/__/__

Take a deep breath, connect with Source and ask:

How do I need to BE to show up as my Ideal Self today?

What do I need to do to show up as my Ideal Self today?

Take a deep breath, connect with Source and ask:

How do I need to BE to show up as my Ideal Self today?

What do I need to do to show up as my Ideal Self today?

Date __/__/__

Take a deep breath, connect with Source and ask:

How do I need to BE to show up as my Ideal Self today?

What do I need to do to show up as my Ideal Self today?

Take a deep breath, connect with Source and ask:

How do I need to BE to show up as my Ideal Self today?

What do I need to do to show up as my Ideal Self today?

Date __/__/__

Take a deep breath, connect with Source and ask:

How do I need to BE to show up as my Ideal Self today?

What do I need to do to show up as my Ideal Self today?

Take a deep breath, connect with Source and ask:

How do I need to BE to show up as my Ideal Self today?

What do I need to do to show up as my Ideal Self today?

Date __/__/__

Take a deep breath, connect with Source and ask:

How do I need to BE to show up as my Ideal Self today?

What do I need to do to show up as my Ideal Self today?

Take a deep breath, connect with Source and ask:

How do I need to BE to show up as my Ideal Self today?

What do I need to do to show up as my Ideal Self today?

Date __/__/__

Take a deep breath, connect with Source and ask:

How do I need to BE to show up as my Ideal Self today?

What do I need to do to show up as my Ideal Self today?

Take a deep breath, connect with Source and ask:

How do I need to BE to show up as my Ideal Self today?

What do I need to do to show up as my Ideal Self today?

Date __/__/__

Take a deep breath, connect with Source and ask:

How do I need to BE to show up as my Ideal Self today?

What do I need to do to show up as my Ideal Self today?

Take a deep breath, connect with Source and ask:

How do I need to BE to show up as my Ideal Self today?

What do I need to do to show up as my Ideal Self today?

Date __/__/__

Take a deep breath, connect with Source and ask:

How do I need to BE to show up as my Ideal Self today?

What do I need to do to show up as my Ideal Self today?

Take a deep breath, connect with Source and ask:

How do I need to BE to show up as my Ideal Self today?

What do I need to do to show up as my Ideal Self today?

Date __/__/__

Take a deep breath, connect with Source and ask:

How do I need to BE to show up as my Ideal Self today?

What do I need to do to show up as my Ideal Self today?

Take a deep breath, connect with Source and ask:

How do I need to BE to show up as my Ideal Self today?

What do I need to do to show up as my Ideal Self today?

Date __/__/__

Take a deep breath, connect with Source and ask:

How do I need to BE to show up as my Ideal Self today?

What do I need to do to show up as my Ideal Self today?

Take a deep breath, connect with Source and ask:

How do I need to BE to show up as my Ideal Self today?

What do I need to do to show up as my Ideal Self today?

Date __/__/__

Take a deep breath, connect with Source and ask:

How do I need to BE to show up as my Ideal Self today?

What do I need to do to show up as my Ideal Self today?

Take a deep breath, connect with Source and ask:

How do I need to BE to show up as my Ideal Self today?

What do I need to do to show up as my Ideal Self today?

Date __/__/__

Take a deep breath, connect with Source and ask:

How do I need to BE to show up as my Ideal Self today?

What do I need to do to show up as my Ideal Self today?

Take a deep breath, connect with Source and ask:

How do I need to BE to show up as my Ideal Self today?

What do I need to do to show up as my Ideal Self today?

Date __/__/__

Take a deep breath, connect with Source and ask:

How do I need to BE to show up as my Ideal Self today?

What do I need to do to show up as my Ideal Self today?

Take a deep breath, connect with Source and ask:

How do I need to BE to show up as my Ideal Self today?

What do I need to do to show up as my Ideal Self today?

Date __/__/__

Take a deep breath, connect with Source and ask:

How do I need to BE to show up as my Ideal Self today?

What do I need to do to show up as my Ideal Self today?

Take a deep breath, connect with Source and ask:

How do I need to BE to show up as my Ideal Self today?

What do I need to do to show up as my Ideal Self today?

Date __/__/__

Take a deep breath, connect with Source and ask:

How do I need to BE to show up as my Ideal Self today?

What do I need to do to show up as my Ideal Self today?

Take a deep breath, connect with Source and ask:

How do I need to BE to show up as my Ideal Self today?

What do I need to do to show up as my Ideal Self today?

Date __/__/__

Take a deep breath, connect with Source and ask:

How do I need to BE to show up as my Ideal Self today?

What do I need to do to show up as my Ideal Self today?

Take a deep breath, connect with Source and ask:

How do I need to BE to show up as my Ideal Self today?

What do I need to do to show up as my Ideal Self today?